Natto

A Beginner's Quick Start Guide and 5-Step Action Plan, With Sample Recipes

copyright © 2024 Isadora Kwon

All rights reserved No part of this book may be reproduced, or stored in a retrieval system, or transmitted in any form or by any means, electronic, mechanical, photocopying, recording, or otherwise, without express written permission of the publisher.

Disclaimer

By reading this disclaimer, you are accepting the terms of the disclaimer in full. If you disagree with this disclaimer, please do not read the guide.

All of the content within this guide is provided for informational and educational purposes only, and should not be accepted as independent medical or other professional advice. The author is not a doctor, physician, nurse, mental health provider, or registered nutritionist/dietician. Therefore, using and reading this guide does not establish any form of a physician-patient relationship.

Always consult with a physician or another qualified health provider with any issues or questions you might have regarding any sort of medical condition. Do not ever disregard any qualified professional medical advice or delay seeking that advice because of anything you have read in this guide. The information in this guide is not intended to be any sort of medical advice and should not be used in lieu of any medical advice by a licensed and qualified medical professional.

The information in this guide has been compiled from a variety of known sources. However, the author cannot attest to or guarantee the accuracy of each source and thus should not be held liable for any errors or omissions.

You acknowledge that the publisher of this guide will not be held liable for any loss or damage of any kind incurred as a result of this guide or the reliance on any information provided within this guide. You acknowledge and agree that you assume all risk and responsibility for any action you undertake in response to the information in this guide.

Using this guide does not guarantee any particular result (e.g., weight loss or a cure). By reading this guide, you acknowledge that there are no guarantees to any specific outcome or results you can expect.

All product names, diet plans, or names used in this guide are for identification purposes only and are the property of their respective owners. The use of these names does not imply endorsement. All other trademarks cited herein are the property of their respective owners.

Where applicable, this guide is not intended to be a substitute for the original work of this diet plan and is, at most, a supplement to the original work for this diet plan and never a direct substitute. This guide is a personal expression of the facts of that diet plan.

Where applicable, persons shown in the cover images are stock photography models and the publisher has obtained the rights to use the images through license agreements with third-party stock image companies.

Table of Contents

Disclaimer	3
Table of Contents	5
Chapter 1: What is Natto?	6
Traditional Methods of Preparation and Fermentation	6
Cultural Significance and Role in Japanese Meals	7
Health Use Cases of Natto	8
How Does Natto Work in The Body?	9
Chapter 2: Health Benefits of Natto	10
Potential Disadvantages of Incorporating Natto	12
Chapter 3: 5-Step Action Plan for Incorporating Natto into Your Diet	14
Step 1: Start Small and Familiarize Yourself with Natto	14
Step 2: Mix Natto with Familiar Foods	16
Step 3: Enhance Natto with Texture and Flavor	17
Step 4: Incorporate Natto into Meals Throughout the Day	19
Step 5: Make Natto a Regular Part of Your Diet	20
Chapter 4: Sample Recipes	22
Natto Avocado Toast Recipe	22
Natto & Tomato Salad Recipe	24
Natto Sushi Rolls Recipe	26
Natto Omelet Recipe	28
Stir-fried Natto Noodles Recipe	30
Natto Miso Soup	32
Natto Pancakes	34
Natto Fried Rice	36
Natto Tacos	38

Natto Smoothie	40
Natto & Veggie Wrap	44
Natto Caesar Salad	46
Natto Onigiri	48
Natto Stir-fry with Tofu	50
Natto & Egg Breakfast Bowl	52
Natto Veggie Burger	54
Natto Spaghetti	56
Conclusion	**58**
FAQs	**60**
What is natto and how is it traditionally prepared?	60
What are the health benefits of consuming natto?	60
How does natto fit into Japanese culture and cuisine?	61
What are some common misconceptions about natto's taste and texture?	61
How can I incorporate natto into my meals?	61
Are there any potential disadvantages or side effects of eating natto?	62
Is making natto at home difficult, and what should I know before trying?	62
Resources and Helpful Links	**63**

Chapter 1: What is Natto?

Natto is a time-honored Japanese delicacy crafted from fermented soybeans, renowned for its distinctive and memorable qualities. Its sticky texture, potent aroma, and unique taste make it an acquired preference for many, yet it is cherished as a staple in Japanese cuisine.

Often served atop steamed rice, natto is a breakfast favorite, complemented by soy sauce, mustard, or green onions to enhance its flavor. Beyond its culinary uses, natto holds cultural significance, representing a piece of Japanese heritage and tradition. Despite its unusual characteristics, it offers a rich source of nutrition and embodies the essence of Japanese gastronomy.

Traditional Methods of Preparation and Fermentation

The traditional methods of preparing and fermenting natto involve several key steps:

1. **Soaking the Soybeans**: The process begins with soaking soybeans in water for an extended period. This step is crucial as it increases the size of the beans and softens them, making them ready for cooking.
2. **Cooking the Soybeans**: After soaking, the soybeans are either steamed or boiled until they reach a soft consistency. This ensures that the beans are adequately prepared for fermentation.
3. **Introducing Bacillus Subtilis**: The transformation of soybeans into natto is achieved by introducing the

Bacillus subtilis bacteria. Traditionally, this was done by wrapping the cooked beans in rice straw, which naturally contains the bacteria. In modern methods, a culture starter containing Bacillus subtilis is often used.
4. **Fermentation**: The wrapped or inoculated soybeans are left to ferment for about 24 to 48 hours. During this time, the bacteria work on the beans, developing the characteristic sticky texture and strong aroma of natto.
5. **Maturation**: After fermentation, the natto is typically stored in a cool place to allow the flavors to mature further, enhancing its taste and texture.

These traditional methods ensure that natto retains its rich flavor and nutritional benefits, making it a staple in Japanese cuisine.

Cultural Significance and Role in Japanese Meals

Natto holds a significant place in Japanese culture and cuisine, celebrated for both its health benefits and its traditional roots. Here's a look at its cultural significance and role in Japanese meals:

1. **Health and Longevity**: Natto is often associated with health and longevity in Japan. It's considered a superfood due to its high protein content and rich supply of vitamins and minerals, particularly vitamin K2, which supports bone health and cardiovascular function. The probiotics in natto also promote digestive health.

2. **Culinary Tradition**: In Japanese cuisine, natto is most commonly consumed as a breakfast item. It's typically served over rice, accompanied by soy sauce, mustard, and chopped green onions. This simple yet nutritious meal is a staple in many Japanese households.
3. **Versatility in Dishes**: Beyond breakfast, natto's versatility allows it to be incorporated into various dishes, such as sushi rolls, omelets, and salads. Its unique flavor and texture add depth to these dishes, making it a popular ingredient in creative culinary applications.
4. **Cultural Heritage**: Natto represents a culinary tradition passed down through generations, reflecting Japan's rich cultural heritage. It is particularly celebrated in regions like Ibaraki Prefecture, known for its natto production, where it is a source of regional pride.
5. **Symbol of Regional Identity**: Despite its growing popularity, natto remains a symbol of regional identity and pride, especially in areas where it has been traditionally produced. This connection to local culture and history enhances its significance beyond just a food item.

Overall, natto is cherished not only for its nutritional benefits but also as a cultural icon that embodies the essence of Japanese culinary and cultural identity.

Health Use Cases of Natto

The consumption of natto has been linked to various health benefits, making it a popular functional food in Japan and around the world. Some potential health use cases of natto include:

1. **Dietary Supplement**: Natto is used as a natural source of vitamin K2 supplements, which are important for various bodily functions.
2. **Functional Food**: It's incorporated into diets as a functional food to support overall wellness, often included in meal plans focused on specific health goals.
3. **Traditional Medicine**: In some cultures, natto is used in traditional medicine practices for its potential health-supporting properties.
4. **Nutritional Enrichment**: It's used to enrich diets with essential nutrients, particularly in vegetarian and vegan meal plans, due to its protein and nutrient content.

Overall, natto's potential health benefits are a significant factor in its widespread consumption and popularity as a traditional Japanese food. Its versatility in usage, whether as a supplement or functional food, has made it an essential component of many diets.

How Does Natto Work in The Body?

Natto, a fermented soybean dish, operates through several mechanisms in the body, primarily due to its rich content of probiotics, nattokinase, and vitamin K2.

1. **Probiotics and Gut Health**: Natto contains beneficial bacteria that contribute to a healthy gut microbiome. These probiotics enhance digestive health by balancing the gut flora, which aids in the breakdown of food, improves nutrient absorption, and supports regular bowel movements. A balanced gut microbiome can also bolster the immune system, as a significant portion of the immune system is housed in the gut.
2. **Nattokinase and Cardiovascular Function**: Nattokinase is a potent enzyme found in natto that plays a crucial role in cardiovascular health. It works by breaking down fibrin, a protein involved in blood clot formation.Nattokinase lowers fibrin levels, which aids in preventing blood clots, thereby enhancing circulation and decreasing the likelihood of developing conditions like deep vein thrombosis and stroke. This enzyme also contributes to lowering blood pressure by enhancing circulation.
3. **Vitamin K2 and Bone Health**: Natto is one of the richest food sources of vitamin K2, which is essential for bone health. Vitamin K2 activates proteins that bind calcium, directing it to the bones and teeth where it is needed, and away from arteries and soft tissues where it could cause damage. This process helps

improve bone density and reduce the risk of fractures and osteoporosis.

Overall, the components of natto work synergistically to support digestive, cardiovascular, and skeletal systems, contributing to overall health and well-being.

Chapter 2: Health Benefits of Natto

Natto is not only a staple in Japanese cuisine, but it also offers numerous health benefits. Here's an overview of some of the potential health benefits of consuming natto regularly:

1. **Heart Health**

Natto, a traditional Japanese food made from fermented soybeans, contains nattokinase, a powerful enzyme that has been studied for its potential heart health benefits. This enzyme may help prevent heart disease by reducing blood clot formation, which can lead to serious cardiovascular issues.

Additionally, nattokinase supports healthy blood pressure levels by promoting proper blood flow and circulation. Including natto in your diet can be a delicious way to enhance your heart health and contribute to your overall well-being.

2. **Bone Health**

Bone health is vital for overall well-being, and one key player in maintaining strong bones is vitamin K2. This essential nutrient plays a crucial role in regulating calcium levels, ensuring that calcium is properly deposited in the bones where it strengthens them, rather than accumulating in the arteries which can lead to health problems.

Adequate vitamin K2 intake helps prevent fractures and supports bone density, making it a significant factor in preventing osteoporosis and promoting long-term skeletal strength. Including vitamin K2-rich foods in your diet, such as fermented products and certain cheeses, can contribute greatly to maintaining bone health and overall vitality.

3. **Gut Health**

As a fermented food, natto is rich in probiotics, which are beneficial bacteria that support gut health. By promoting a healthy balance of gut bacteria, natto can enhance digestion and improve nutrient absorption.

This unique Japanese dish not only helps maintain a thriving microbiome but also contributes to overall well-being by potentially boosting the immune system and reducing inflammation. Including natto in your diet can be a delicious way to support your gut health.

4. **Anti-inflammatory Properties**

Natto, a traditional Japanese fermented soybean dish, may help reduce inflammation in the body due to its rich content of bioactive compounds. These compounds, including nattokinase and various vitamins, play a crucial role in modulating the body's inflammatory response.

This anti-inflammatory effect is beneficial for overall health, as it can help manage chronic conditions such as arthritis, heart disease, and even metabolic disorders. By incorporating natto into your diet, you may not only enjoy its unique flavor but also support your body's efforts to combat inflammation and promote better health.

5. **<u>Nutrient-rich</u>**

This food is not only high in protein, making it a great option for muscle repair and growth, but it also contains polyunsaturated fats. These healthy fats can play a significant role in lowering LDL cholesterol levels, which is essential for maintaining heart health. By incorporating nutrient-rich foods into your diet, you can help reduce the risk of heart disease and stroke, ultimately promoting better overall wellness.

Incorporating natto into your diet can offer many health benefits, making it a valuable addition to vegan meal plans. Natto is also rich in antioxidants and contains essential vitamins and minerals such as iron, magnesium, and potassium.

Potential Disadvantages of Incorporating Natto

While natto offers several health benefits, there are a few potential disadvantages to consider before adding it to your diet.

1. **Acquired Taste and Texture**

Natto has a distinct, pungent odor and slimy texture that some individuals may find off-putting. Those unaccustomed to these characteristics might require time to adjust to its unique sensory profile. Despite this, many find that its health benefits, such as improved digestion and heart health, make it worthwhile to incorporate into their diet.

2. **Potential Allergies**

As a soy product, natto can trigger allergic reactions in individuals with soy allergies. It's essential for these individuals to consult with a healthcare professional before adding natto to their diet. However, for those without allergies, natto offers a rich source of protein and essential nutrients.

3. **High Sodium Content**

Some varieties of natto may contain added salt, contributing to an increased sodium intake. Monitoring portion sizes can help mitigate this issue, allowing individuals to enjoy the cardiovascular benefits of natto's high vitamin K2 content without excessive sodium consumption.

4. **Fermentation Complexity**

The fermentation process used to make natto can be complex and time-consuming if one chooses to prepare it at home. Despite this, the commercially available versions provide a convenient option that retains the myriad of health benefits associated with fermented foods, such as enhanced gut flora.

5. **Limited Availability**

In certain regions, natto might be difficult to find, limiting immediate access. Nonetheless, as interest in global cuisines grows, more stores are beginning to stock this nutritious food, making its health-promoting qualities more accessible.

While there are some challenges associated with incorporating natto into a diet, the nutritional advantages, such as its probiotic properties and nutrient density, significantly outweigh these disadvantages.

Chapter 3: 5-Step Action Plan for Incorporating Natto into Your Diet

When it comes to adding new foods to your diet, it's essential to have a plan in place. This approach helps establish healthy habits and ensures that natto is incorporated effectively into your daily routine. Here are five simple steps to help you get started on incorporating natto into your diet:

Step 1: Start Small and Familiarize Yourself with Natto

1. **Understanding Natto and Its Benefits**

Begin your journey by learning about natto's incredible health benefits. Natto is a traditional Japanese food made from fermented soybeans, known for being rich in probiotics, which support gut health, and vitamin K2, essential for bone strength. Embrace the idea that while natto has a distinctive flavor and aroma, it offers unparalleled nutritional advantages that can enhance your overall well-being.

2. **Where to Buy Natto**

You can find natto in the refrigerated section of Asian grocery stores or order it online from specialty food websites. Look for small packs, usually sold in sets of three or four, which are perfect for beginners. Opting for smaller quantities allows you to sample natto without committing to a large purchase.

3. **How to Store Natto**

Once you've purchased natto, store it in your refrigerator to maintain its freshness. It typically has a relatively long shelf life due to the fermentation process, but always check the expiration date on the package. Keeping natto refrigerated ensures it retains its distinct texture and flavor until you're ready to enjoy it.

4. **Tasting Natto for the First Time**

Prepare yourself for natto's unique characteristics. Its texture is sticky and somewhat stringy, and the smell is often described as strong and pungent. To ease into the experience, try a small spoonful on its own. Focus on the earthy and slightly nutty flavor profile, which might take a little getting used to but can become enjoyable over time.

5. **Overcoming Initial Hesitations**

It's normal to feel hesitant about trying something new. Remind yourself of natto's impressive health benefits and the culinary adventure it offers. Approach this with an open mind, viewing it as an opportunity to expand your palate and discover new tastes.

Remember, many people have grown to appreciate and even love natto after their first few tries. Take it one step at a time and trust your taste buds to adapt. You're embarking on a rewarding culinary journey that could lead to a healthier and more diverse diet. Embrace each bite as a step toward better health and culinary curiosity.

Step 2: Mix Natto with Familiar Foods

1. **Combining Natto with Rice**

Start by incorporating natto into a warm bowl of rice, a classic pairing that softens natto's powerful taste. The warm rice helps to mellow the flavor and provides a comforting base that balances natto's texture. To prepare, cook your rice until fluffy, then let it cool slightly before stirring in a portion of natto. This combination not only enhances the taste but also increases your meal's fiber content and nutritional value.

2. **Enhancing Flavor with Soy Sauce and Mustard**

Adding a splash of soy sauce or a dab of mustard can significantly improve natto's palatability. Soy sauce introduces a savory depth with its salty and umami notes, while mustard adds a tangy zest that complements natto's earthy tones. Mix these condiments directly into the natto before adding it to your rice or other dishes. Start with small amounts and adjust according to your taste preferences.

3. **Incorporating Natto into Familiar Dishes**

Try mixing natto into dishes you already love. Stir it into a vegetable stir-fry, blend it into a miso soup, or add it to your ramen bowl. These familiar contexts can make natto feel less intimidating and more like a natural addition to your meals. The key is to integrate natto into dishes where its texture and flavor can enhance rather than overpower the other ingredients.

4. **Experimenting with Additional Ingredients**

Feel free to explore other ingredients that can complement natto. Chopped scallions, for example, add a fresh crunch and mild onion flavor, while toasted sesame seeds provide a nutty aroma and crunchy texture. You might also try mixing in kimchi for a spicy kick or avocado for a creamy contrast. These additions not only diversify the flavors but also increase the nutritional benefits of your meal.

Experimentation is crucial in finding what works best for your palate. Don't hesitate to try different combinations and adjust the flavors to suit your taste. Whether you prefer a milder approach with rice and soy sauce or a bolder mix with spicy condiments, the aim is to make natto a sustainable and enjoyable part of your diet. Remember, your taste preferences are unique, so let your creativity guide you in creating meals that you'll look forward to enjoying.

Step 3: Enhance Natto with Texture and Flavor

1. **Adding Crunch with Green Onions**

Incorporate chopped green onions into your natto for a burst of freshness and a satisfying crunch. The mild onion flavor of green onions complements natto's earthy taste, creating a well-rounded flavor profile. To prepare, finely slice the green onions and sprinkle them over your natto just before serving. This simple addition not only enhances the dish's flavor but also adds a pop of color, making your meal more visually appealing.

2. **Incorporating Sesame Seeds for Nutty Aromas**

Sprinkling toasted sesame seeds over natto can introduce a delightful nutty aroma and additional texture. The seeds provide a gentle crunch and pair well with the umami flavors of natto. To prepare, lightly toast the sesame seeds in a dry skillet over medium heat until golden brown, then scatter them over your natto. This subtle enhancement can significantly elevate your eating experience, making each bite more enjoyable.

3. **Enhancing Flavor with Nori**

Shredded nori, or seaweed, can add a savory umami boost to your natto dishes. The briny taste of nori complements natto's unique flavor and adds a chewy texture that contrasts nicely with its stickiness. Simply tear or cut nori sheets into small strips and mix them with your natto before serving. This addition not only enriches the flavor but also introduces beneficial minerals from the seaweed.

4. **Exploring Additional Ingredients**

Feel free to experiment with other ingredients such as kimchi for a spicy and tangy kick, or avocado for a smooth, creamy contrast. These components can balance natto's flavor and texture, making it more appealing to your palate. Try adding a dash of lemon juice for brightness or a sprinkle of chili flakes for heat, tailoring your dish to your taste preferences.

Encourage your creativity by trying different flavor combinations and discovering which ones resonate with you. The goal is to personalize your natto experience, making it an enjoyable part of your diet. Don't hesitate to adjust ingredients and proportions based on what you find most satisfying. As you explore these options, you'll likely uncover unique pairings that transform natto into a dish you truly enjoy.

Step 4: Incorporate Natto into Meals Throughout the Day

1. **Breakfast: Natto Toast**

Start your day with a nutritious twist by adding natto to your breakfast routine. Natto toast is both simple and delicious. Begin by toasting a slice of whole-grain bread until crispy. Spread a light layer of avocado or cream cheese on the toast, then top it with a generous scoop of natto.

Add slices of ripe tomato or a sprinkle of sesame seeds for extra flavor. This combination provides a healthy dose of proteins and fibers to kickstart your morning, while the avocado or cream cheese helps balance natto's bold flavor.

2. **Lunch: Natto Salad**

For a refreshing lunch option, toss natto into your salad for a protein-rich meal. Start with a base of leafy greens such as spinach or kale. Add a mix of colorful vegetables like cherry tomatoes, cucumbers, and bell peppers. Top your salad with natto and a sprinkle of chopped green onions or nori strips for an extra burst of flavor.

Dress with a light vinaigrette made from soy sauce, rice vinegar, and a touch of sesame oil. This meal not only enhances your vitamin intake but also introduces a savory element that complements the crisp vegetables.

3. **Dinner: Natto Sushi Rolls**

Incorporate natto into your dinner by making natto sushi rolls. Lay a sheet of nori flat on a bamboo sushi mat, spread a thin layer of sushi rice over it, leaving an inch at the top edge. Add a line of natto along with slices of cucumber and avocado.

Roll the sushi tightly, using the bamboo mat to shape it. Slice it into bite-sized pieces and serve with soy sauce and pickled ginger. These rolls provide a delightful mix of textures and flavors, with natto adding a distinct umami depth to the roll.

4. **Exploring Different Meal Contexts**

The versatility of natto allows you to integrate it into various meal contexts, making it a valuable addition to your diet. Whether you prefer it as a topping, mixed into dishes, or as a main component, natto can enhance the nutritional profile of any meal. Experiment with incorporating natto in diverse dishes like omelets for breakfast, wraps for lunch, or even as a pizza topping for dinner.

By trying natto in different meal settings, you open the door to culinary creativity and enhance your dietary variety. Embrace the flexibility natto offers and enjoy discovering how it can complement and elevate your everyday meals. As you explore these versatile uses, you'll likely find new, exciting ways to appreciate natto's unique flavor and health benefits.

Step 5: Make Natto a Regular Part of Your Diet

1. **Setting a Routine**

To seamlessly incorporate natto into your regular diet, start by establishing a routine. Choose specific days of the week to include natto in your meals, such as every Monday and Thursday. This predictability helps you build a habit and ensures that natto becomes a consistent part of your dietary intake. Schedule natto meals at times when you can enjoy them most, perhaps during breakfast when you have time to prepare a natto toast or at dinner with a natto sushi roll.

2. **Tracking Your Progress**

Keep a simple journal or use a meal-tracking app to note your natto consumption. Record how you feel after meals, any changes in digestion, and your taste preferences as you experiment with different recipes. This practice not only helps you stay committed but also allows you to observe the benefits of integrating natto into your diet over time. Tracking progress can also motivate you to try new recipes and maintain variety in your meals.

3. **Gradually Increasing Consumption**

Start with small portions of natto and gradually increase the amount as you become more accustomed to its flavor and texture. This gradual increase helps your taste buds adjust while also allowing your digestive system to acclimate to the new food. Begin by adding natto to one meal per week, then slowly incorporate it into additional meals as you grow more comfortable.

4. Health Benefits of Regular Natto Consumption

Regular consumption of natto offers numerous health benefits. It is rich in probiotics, which can improve digestion and gut health. The vitamin K2 found in natto plays a vital role in promoting bone and heart health by helping prevent calcium build-up in arteries. Additionally, natto is high in protein and fiber, which can help maintain energy levels and support muscle health.

5. Encouragement for Consistency

Consistency is key when adopting any dietary change. Remind yourself of the health benefits you're gaining from regular natto consumption. These include better digestion, enhanced nutrient absorption, and improved cardiovascular health. Surround yourself with supportive resources, such as online communities or recipe blogs, to keep your motivation high. Celebrate small milestones, like trying a new natto recipe each week, to maintain enthusiasm and commitment.

To keep the momentum, set personal goals for your natto journey, such as mastering a new natto dish monthly or sharing a meal with friends to introduce them to natto. Stay curious and keep exploring different ways to enjoy natto, ensuring it remains an exciting and beneficial part of your diet. By committing to these practices, you'll make natto a regular, healthy part of your lifestyle, enjoying both its unique flavors and its numerous health benefits over time.

Chapter 4: Sample Recipes

We've included a few sample recipes to help you get started on your natto journey. These are just some ideas, so feel free to experiment and find what works best for you!

Natto Avocado Toast Recipe

Ingredients:

- 2 slices of whole-grain or sourdough bread
- 1 ripe avocado
- 1 pack natto (about 50 grams)
- 1 tablespoon soy sauce or the sauce included with the natto
- 1 tablespoon lemon juice
- Salt and pepper to taste
- 1 tablespoon olive oil or butter for toasting
- 1 small red radish, thinly sliced (optional, for garnish)
- 1 tablespoon chopped chives or green onions
- Toasted sesame seeds (optional, for garnish)

Instructions:

1. **Prepare the Bread:**
    - Heat olive oil or butter in a skillet over medium heat. Toast the bread slices until golden and crisp, about 2-3 minutes per side. Alternatively, use a toaster for convenience.
2. **Make the Avocado Spread:**

- In a bowl, mash the avocado with a fork. Add lemon juice, salt, and pepper, mixing until smooth and creamy. Adjust seasoning to taste.
3. **Prepare the Natto:**
    - Open the natto pack and mix it well with the soy sauce or the included sauce until it becomes creamy. This step helps enhance its flavor and texture.
4. **Assemble the Toast:**
    - Spread a generous layer of avocado mixture over each slice of toasted bread. Top with a spoonful of prepared natto, spreading it evenly.
5. **Garnish:**
    - Sprinkle chopped chives or green onions over the top. For added crunch and color, garnish with thinly sliced radish and toasted sesame seeds.
6. **Serve:**
    - Serve immediately to enjoy the textures and flavors at their best.

Tips for Preparation:

- **Natto Mixing:** Stirring natto thoroughly before use ensures even distribution of its flavor.
- **Avocado Ripeness:** Use a perfectly ripe avocado for the best texture and taste; it should yield slightly when pressed.
- **Bread Choice:** Whole-grain or sourdough bread provides a sturdy base and complements the creamy toppings well.

Serving Suggestions:

Natto Avocado Toast is best enjoyed fresh, paired with a cup of hot coffee or a refreshing smoothie. It makes a delightful breakfast or a quick, healthy snack any time of day. Experiment with additional toppings like sliced tomatoes or a sprinkle of chili flakes for a personalized touch. Enjoy exploring this fusion of tastes and textures!

Natto & Tomato Salad Recipe

Ingredients:

- 1 pack natto (about 50 grams)
- 2 large ripe tomatoes, chopped
- 1 small cucumber, thinly sliced
- 1/4 red onion, finely sliced
- 1/4 cup fresh basil leaves, torn
- 2 tablespoons olive oil
- 1 tablespoon rice vinegar
- 1 teaspoon soy sauce
- Salt and pepper to taste
- 1 tablespoon toasted sesame seeds (optional)
- Mixed salad greens for serving

Instructions:

1. **Prepare the Natto:**
    - Open the natto pack and mix it well with the included sauce or 1 teaspoon of soy sauce until it becomes creamy, which helps enhance its flavor and texture.

2. **Chop the Vegetables:**
   - In a big bowl, mix together the diced tomatoes, cucumber slices, and red onion slices, tossing gently to combine.
3. **Dress the Salad:**
   - In a small bowl, blend the olive oil, rice vinegar, salt, and pepper until well combined. Drizzle this dressing over the vegetables and toss until they are evenly coated.
4. **Assemble the Salad:**
   - Add the prepared natto to the vegetable mix and gently fold together. Be careful not to overmix, as you want to keep the tomatoes intact.
5. **Add Fresh Herbs:**
   - Gently incorporate the torn basil leaves into the salad for a burst of fresh flavor.
6. **Serve:**
   - Arrange mixed salad greens on a serving platter or individual plates. Spoon the natto and tomato mixture over the greens. Garnish with toasted sesame seeds for an added crunch and nutty flavor.

Tips for Preparation:

- **Natto Handling:** Stirring natto thoroughly before adding it to the salad helps to evenly distribute its distinctive flavor.
- **Tomato Selection:** Use ripe, firm tomatoes for the best texture and sweetness.

- **Herb Substitution:** If basil is unavailable, substitute with fresh cilantro or parsley.

Serving Suggestions:

This Natto & Tomato Salad pairs well with a simple grilled fish or chicken dish, making it a versatile addition to any meal. Enjoy it with a light, chilled white wine or iced green tea for a refreshing dining experience. Explore the delightful combination of flavors and textures that this salad offers!

Natto Sushi Rolls Recipe

Ingredients:

- 2 cups sushi rice
- 2 1/2 cups water
- 1/4 cup rice vinegar
- 1 tablespoon sugar
- 1 teaspoon salt
- 4 sheets of nori (seaweed)
- 1 pack natto (about 50 grams)
- 1 cucumber, julienned
- 1 avocado, sliced
- Soy sauce packet from natto (or 1 tablespoon soy sauce)
- 1 tablespoon pickled ginger, finely chopped
- Wasabi and soy sauce for serving
- Pickled ginger for garnish

Instructions:

1. **Prepare the Sushi Rice:**
   - Rinse the sushi rice under cold water until the water runs clear. Place rice and water into a rice cooker and follow the manufacturer's guidelines to cook. After cooking, move the rice into a large bowl.
2. **Add Flavor to the Rice:**
   - In a small dish, combine rice vinegar, sugar, and salt until they dissolve. Drizzle this mixture over the warm rice and gently fold it in to ensure even seasoning. Let the rice cool to room temperature.
3. **Prepare the Natto:**
   - Open the natto pack and mix it well with the included soy sauce packet or regular soy sauce to enhance its flavor and texture.
4. **Set Up for Rolling:**
   - Place a bamboo sushi mat on a clean surface. Lay a sheet of nori on the mat, shiny side down.
5. **Assemble the Sushi Roll:**
   - Wet your hands to prevent sticking. Spread a thin layer of sushi rice over the nori, leaving about 1 inch at the top edge uncovered.
   - Arrange a row of natto, cucumber, avocado, and a sprinkle of pickled ginger across the rice, about 1 inch from the bottom edge.
6. **Roll the Sushi:**
   - Starting from the bottom edge, use the bamboo mat to roll the sushi tightly into a log, applying gentle pressure to keep the roll firm. Seal the

edge by moistening the uncovered nori with a little water.

7. **Slice and Serve:**
   - Use a sharp knife to slice the roll into 6-8 even pieces, cleaning the knife between cuts for the best results.
   - Arrange the pieces on a serving platter and garnish with pickled ginger. Serve with wasabi and soy sauce on the side.

Tips for Preparation:

- **Rice Handling:** Ensure the rice is adequately cooled before assembling the rolls to prevent the nori from becoming soggy.
- **Natto Flavor:** Mixing natto with soy sauce or included packet helps to mellow its strong flavor.
- **Rolling Technique:** Practice makes perfect. If the roll isn't tight enough, gently re-roll it using the bamboo mat.

Serving Suggestions:

Natto Sushi Rolls are a versatile dish that can be enjoyed as a main or as part of a larger sushi spread. Pair with miso soup or a simple seaweed salad to round out the meal. Enjoy experimenting with this fusion of textures and flavors in the comfort of your home!

Natto Omelet Recipe

This Natto Omelet brings a savory, nutritious twist to a breakfast classic. Combining the unique flavor of natto with fluffy eggs, this dish is both simple and satisfying, perfect for those looking to explore new ingredients in their cooking repertoire.

Ingredients:

- 3 large eggs
- 1 pack natto (about 50 grams)
- 1 tablespoon soy sauce
- 1 tablespoon milk or water
- 1 tablespoon vegetable oil or butter
- 1 small onion, finely chopped
- 1/2 cup baby spinach leaves
- 1/4 cup shredded cheese (optional)
- 1 green onion, sliced
- Salt and pepper to taste
- Toasted sesame seeds (optional, for garnish)
- Fresh herbs (e.g., cilantro or parsley) for garnish

Instructions:

1. **Prepare the Eggs:**
    - In a bowl, crack the eggs and add the soy sauce and milk (or water). Whisk together until well combined and slightly frothy. Set aside.
2. **Prepare the Natto:**
    - Open the natto pack and mix it with the included sauce until it becomes creamy. This will enhance its flavor and improve its texture.
3. **Cook the Aromatics:**

- Heat the oil or butter in a non-stick skillet over medium heat. Add the chopped onion and sauté for about 2 minutes until it becomes translucent and fragrant.

4. **Add Spinach and Natto:**
   - Add the spinach to the skillet and cook until just wilted, about 1 minute. Stir in the prepared natto, mixing well with the onions and spinach.

5. **Cook the Omelet:**
   - Pour the egg mixture over the vegetables and natto in the skillet. Tilt the pan slightly to ensure even distribution. Cook over medium heat until the edges start to set, about 2-3 minutes.

6. **Add Cheese (Optional):**
   - If using cheese, sprinkle it over one half of the omelet. Allow it to melt slightly.

7. **Fold and Finish:**
   - Carefully fold the omelet in half and cook for an additional 1-2 minutes until it is fully set but remains soft on the inside.

8. **Serve:**
   - Slide the omelet onto a plate. Garnish with sliced green onions, toasted sesame seeds, and fresh herbs for an extra touch of flavor and color.

Tips for Preparation:

- **Natto Handling:** Mixing natto with its sauce before adding it to the omelet helps to mellow its strong flavor and ensures even distribution.
- **Cooking Control:** Keep the heat at medium to prevent the omelet from browning too much or cooking unevenly.
- **Customization:** Feel free to add other fillings such as mushrooms, bell peppers, or tomatoes for added variety and nutrition.

Serving Suggestions:

Serve the Natto Omelet warm, alongside a crisp salad or a slice of whole-grain toast for a balanced meal. A cup of green tea complements the flavors nicely, making for a delightful breakfast or brunch option.

Explore this omelet recipe to discover how natto can bring a new dimension to your morning meal!

Stir-fried Natto Noodles Recipe

Ingredients:

- 200 grams of udon or soba noodles
- 1 pack natto (about 50 grams)
- 1 tablespoon vegetable oil
- 2 cloves garlic, minced
- 1 small onion, thinly sliced

- 1 cup mixed vegetables (such as bell peppers, carrots, and snap peas), julienned
- 2 tablespoons soy sauce
- 1 tablespoon oyster sauce (or vegetarian substitute)
- 1 teaspoon sesame oil
- 2 green onions, chopped
- 1 tablespoon toasted sesame seeds (optional)
- Red chili flakes or sliced chili (optional for heat)

Instructions:

1. **Cook the Noodles:**
   - Heat a pot of water to boiling and prepare the noodles following the package directions until they reach al dente texture. Drain them and rinse with cold water to halt further cooking. Put them aside.
2. **Prepare the Natto:**
   - Open the natto pack and mix it well with the included sauce until it becomes slightly creamy. This helps enhance its flavor and improves the texture.
3. **Stir-fry the Aromatics:**
   - Heat the vegetable oil in a large skillet or wok over medium-high heat. Add the minced garlic and sliced onion, and stir-fry for about 2 minutes until fragrant and the onion begins to soften.
4. **Add Vegetables:**

    - Add the mixed vegetables to the skillet and stir-fry for 3-4 minutes, or until they are just tender yet still crisp.
5. **Incorporate the Natto and Noodles:**
    - Add the prepared natto and cooked noodles to the skillet. Toss well to combine all the ingredients.
6. **Season the Noodles:**
    - Pour in the soy sauce, oyster sauce, and sesame oil. Stir everything together and cook for an additional 2-3 minutes, ensuring the noodles are heated through and well-coated with the sauce.
7. **Finish and Serve:**
    - Add the chopped green onions and toss once more before removing the skillet from the heat.
    - Serve the stir-fried natto noodles hot, garnished with toasted sesame seeds and a sprinkle of red chili flakes for added heat, if desired.

Tips for Preparation:

- **Natto Handling:** Stirring the natto well before use helps distribute its flavor evenly throughout the dish.
- **Noodle Choice:** Udon and soba noodles both work well, but feel free to use any noodle variety you prefer.
- **Vegetable Variation:** Customize the dish with your choice of vegetables; mushrooms and broccoli are excellent additions.

Serving Suggestions:

Stir-fried Natto Noodles can be a standalone meal or paired with a side of steamed dumplings or miso soup for a more complete dining experience. Enjoy exploring this nutritious and flavorful dish!

Natto Miso Soup

Ingredients:

- 4 cups dashi stock (or substitute with vegetable broth for a vegetarian version)
- 3 tablespoons miso paste (white or yellow)
- 1 pack natto (about 50 grams)
- 1 block tofu, cut into small cubes
- 1 cup wakame seaweed, rehydrated and drained
- 2 green onions, finely chopped
- 1 tablespoon soy sauce
- 1 teaspoon sesame oil
- 1 tablespoon toasted sesame seeds (optional)
- Fresh ginger, grated (optional for garnish)

Instructions:

1. **Get the Dashi Stock Ready:**
   - In a medium-sized pot, slowly warm the dashi stock over medium heat until it begins to simmer. If you are using vegetable broth instead, follow the same procedure.
2. **Add Tofu and Wakame:**
   - Add the tofu cubes and softened wakame seaweed into the stock while it continues to simmer. Allow them to cook for approximately

3-5 minutes until the tofu is thoroughly warmed.
3. **Incorporate the Natto:**
   - Open the natto pack and mix it with the included sauce to enhance its flavor. Stir the natto into the pot, ensuring it is well distributed in the soup.
4. **Add Miso Paste:**
   - Reduce the heat to avoid boiling, since boiling can change the taste of miso. Take the miso paste and put it in a small bowl, then mix in a small amount of hot broth to dissolve. Once it's smooth, return it to the pot.
5. **Season the Soup:**
   - Stir in the soy sauce and sesame oil. Taste and adjust the seasoning if necessary.
6. **Finish and Serve:**
   - Add the chopped green onions to the soup just before serving to retain their vibrant color and fresh flavor.
   - Ladle the soup into bowls and sprinkle with toasted sesame seeds and grated ginger for an extra touch of flavor, if desired.

Tips for Preparation:

- **Natto Handling:** Stirring the natto well before adding it to the soup helps to improve its texture and evenly distribute its unique flavor.

- **Miso Paste:** Always dissolve miso paste in a small amount of liquid before adding it to the pot to ensure an even distribution.
- **Customization:** Feel free to add vegetables like mushrooms or carrots for added nutrition and texture.

Serving Suggestions:

Natto Miso Soup is best served hot as a starter or a light meal. Pair it with steamed rice or a simple salad to complement its flavors. For those who enjoy a bit of heat, a dash of chili oil can provide an exciting kick.

Natto Pancakes

Ingredients:

- 1 cup of plain flour
- 1 tablespoon of sugar
- 1 teaspoon of baking powder
- 1/2 teaspoon of baking soda
- 1/4 teaspoon of salt
- 1 large egg
- 3/4 cup of milk
- 2 tablespoons of melted butter, with extra for cooking
- 1 teaspoon of soy sauce
- 1/2 cup of natto (around 1 pack)
- 1 green onion, finely chopped
- 1 tablespoon of toasted sesame seeds (optional)
- Extra soy sauce or ponzu sauce for serving
- Fresh herbs such as cilantro or shiso leaves for garnish

Instructions:

1. **Prepare the Dry Ingredients:**
   - In a medium bowl, mix the flour, sugar, baking powder, baking soda, and salt thoroughly with a whisk.
2. **Mix the Wet Ingredients:**
   - In a separate bowl, whisk the egg before adding the milk, melted butter, and soy sauce, blending until smooth.
3. **Combine the Mixtures:**
   - Pour the wet ingredients into the dry ingredients and gently mix them together until just combined. Be careful not to overmix; a few lumps are okay.
4. **Add Natto:**
   - Open the natto pack and stir it with the included sauce for better texture. Add the natto and chopped green onion to the batter, folding them in gently.
5. **Cook the Pancakes:**
   - Warm a non-stick skillet or griddle over medium heat and gently coat it with a bit of butter.
   - For each pancake, ladle approximately 1/4 cup of batter onto the skillet.
   - Cook for about 2-3 minutes on one side, until bubbles form on the surface and the edges start to look set. Flip and cook for another 2-3 minutes until golden brown and cooked through.

6. **Serve:**
    - Transfer the cooked pancakes to a plate and keep them warm while you cook the remaining batter.
    - Sprinkle with toasted sesame seeds if desired, and drizzle with additional soy sauce or ponzu sauce.
    - Garnish with fresh herbs for a touch of color and freshness.

Tips for Preparation:

- **Natto Selection:** For those new to natto, start with a milder variety to gradually acquire a taste for its distinct flavor.
- **Texture:** If you prefer a smoother texture, lightly mash the natto before adding it to the batter.
- **Cooking Tip:** Ensure the pan is well-heated before adding the batter to achieve a nice, golden exterior.
- **Customization:** Feel free to add other ingredients like shredded cheese or chopped vegetables for added flavor and nutrition.

Serving Suggestions:

Natto pancakes are best enjoyed fresh and warm. Pair them with a side of miso soup or a light salad for a complete meal. For a touch of sweetness, a drizzle of honey or maple syrup can add an interesting contrast to the savory flavors.

Natto Fried Rice

Ingredients:

- 2 cups of cooked jasmine or basmati rice, ideally from the previous day
- 1 pack of natto, approximately 50 grams
- 2 tablespoons of soy sauce
- 2 tablespoons of vegetable oil
- 2 eggs, whisked
- 1 small onion, finely chopped
- 1 garlic clove, finely minced
- 1 small carrot, finely diced
- 1/2 cup of thawed frozen peas
- 2 green onions, sliced thinly
- Salt and pepper, as desired
- 1 tablespoon of sesame oil
- Toasted sesame seeds for garnish (optional)

Instructions:

1. **Prepare the Natto:**
    - Open the natto pack and mix it well with the soy sauce until it becomes creamy. This enhances its flavor and makes it easier to incorporate into the fried rice.
2. **Cook the Eggs:**
    - Warm 1 tablespoon of vegetable oil in a large skillet or wok over medium-high heat. Pour in the beaten eggs and cook them, stirring gently, until they are just firm. Take them out of the skillet and keep them aside.

3. **Sauté the Vegetables:**
    - In the same pan, pour in the rest of the tablespoon of oil. Cook the diced onion and garlic for roughly 2 minutes until they release their aroma. Incorporate the chopped carrot and continue cooking for an additional 3-4 minutes until it becomes tender.
4. **Fry the Rice:**
    - Increase the heat to high and add the day-old rice to the skillet. Stir-fry for about 3-5 minutes, breaking up any clumps, until the rice is heated through and slightly crispy.
5. **Combine Ingredients:**
    - Add the scrambled eggs, thawed peas, and prepared natto to the skillet. Stir everything together until well mixed and heated through, about 2-3 minutes.
6. **Season and Garnish:**
    - Drizzle the sesame oil over the fried rice and add salt and pepper to taste. Stir in the green onions and mix well. Garnish with toasted sesame seeds if desired.
7. **Serve:**
    - Serve hot, either as a main dish or a side. Enjoy the unique fusion of flavors and textures!

Tips for Preparation:

- **Rice Prep:** Using day-old rice helps prevent the fried rice from becoming mushy. If freshly cooked rice is

used, spread it out on a baking sheet to cool and dry slightly before frying.
- **Natto Handling:** Stirring natto thoroughly with soy sauce before adding it to the dish ensures even flavor distribution.
- **Vegetable Variations:** Feel free to add or substitute other vegetables like bell peppers or corn for added variety.

Serving Suggestions:

Natto Fried Rice pairs well with a simple side salad or miso soup for a complete meal. It's a versatile dish that can be customized with your favorite vegetables or proteins. Enjoy this delightful combination of flavors with a glass of iced green tea or a light beer for an added treat!

Natto Tacos

Ingredients:

- 1 pack natto (about 50 grams)
- 8 small corn tortillas
- 1 tablespoon soy sauce
- 2 tablespoons vegetable oil
- 1 cup shredded lettuce
- 1/2 cup cherry tomatoes, quartered
- 1/4 cup red onion, finely chopped
- 1 avocado, sliced
- 1/4 cup cilantro leaves
- 1 lime, cut into wedges
- Salt and pepper to taste

- Hot sauce or salsa (optional, for serving)

Instructions:

1. **Prepare the Natto:**
   - Open the natto pack and mix it thoroughly with the soy sauce until creamy. This enhances the flavor and makes it easier to spread on the tortillas.
2. **Warm the Tortillas:**
   - Heat a skillet over medium-high heat. Add a teaspoon of oil and warm each tortilla for about 30 seconds on each side until soft and pliable. Keep them covered with a clean towel to stay warm.
3. **Assemble the Tacos:**
   - Spread a small spoonful of the prepared natto onto each tortilla. Top with shredded lettuce, cherry tomatoes, and red onion.
4. **Add Avocado and Herbs:**
   - Place avocado slices on top and sprinkle with fresh cilantro leaves. Season with salt and pepper to taste.
5. **Serve:**
   - Arrange the tacos on a serving platter and garnish with lime wedges. Drizzle with hot sauce or add salsa if desired.

Tips for Preparation:

- **Natto Mixing:** Ensure natto is well mixed with soy sauce for even flavor distribution.

- **Tortilla Handling:** Keep tortillas warm and soft by covering them with a towel after heating.
- **Flavor Boost:** A squeeze of fresh lime juice adds a refreshing zing to the tacos.

Serving Suggestions:

Natto Tacos are perfect for a light lunch or dinner. Pair them with a side of Mexican rice or a simple black bean salad to round out the meal. Enjoy with a chilled beverage, like a citrusy margarita or sparkling water with lime, for a refreshing complement to the flavors. Let your taste buds explore this exciting fusion of ingredients!

Natto Smoothie

Ingredients:

- 1 pack natto (about 50 grams)
- 1 ripe banana
- 1/2 cup frozen berries (such as blueberries or strawberries)
- 1/2 cup plain yogurt or dairy-free alternative
- 1 tablespoon honey or maple syrup (adjust to taste)
- 1/2 cup almond milk or preferred milk
- 1 tablespoon chia seeds (optional)
- Ice cubes (optional, for a thicker consistency)
- Fresh mint leaves (optional, for garnish)

Instructions:

1. **Prepare the Natto:**

- Open the natto pack and stir it well to achieve a smooth, creamy texture. This helps it blend evenly into the smoothie.

2. **Blend the Ingredients:**
   - In a blender, combine the prepared natto, banana, frozen berries, yogurt, honey, and almond milk. Add chia seeds for an extra nutritional boost if desired.
3. **Adjust Consistency:**
   - Blend on high until smooth and creamy. For a thicker smoothie, add a few ice cubes and blend again until the desired consistency is reached.
4. **Taste and Adjust:**
   - Taste the smoothie and add more honey or maple syrup if additional sweetness is needed.
5. **Serve:**
   - Pour the smoothie into a glass and garnish with fresh mint leaves if desired. Serve immediately to enjoy its fresh flavors.

Tips for Preparation:

- **Natto Handling:** Thoroughly stirring natto before blending ensures it mixes well with other ingredients.
- **Fruit Selection:** Use ripe bananas for natural sweetness and avoid overpowering the natto flavor.
- **Sweetness Level:** Adjust the amount of honey or maple syrup to your liking, especially if using unsweetened yogurt.

Serving Suggestions:

Enjoy this Natto Smoothie as a breakfast alternative or a midday pick-me-up. Pair it with a handful of nuts or a light pastry for a more substantial meal. It's a delicious way to incorporate natto into your diet while enjoying the refreshing taste of fruits. Experiment with different berries or add a scoop of protein powder for added nutrition.

Natto Pizza

Ingredients:

- 1 pre-made pizza crust or homemade dough
- 1 pack natto (about 50 grams)
- 1/4 cup soy sauce
- 1 cup mozzarella cheese, shredded
- 1/2 cup tomato sauce
- 1 small onion, thinly sliced
- 1/2 bell pepper, thinly sliced
- 1/4 cup mushrooms, sliced
- 1/4 cup cherry tomatoes, halved
- 2 tablespoons olive oil
- Fresh basil leaves for garnish
- Salt and pepper to taste
- Red pepper flakes (optional, for a spicy kick)

Instructions:

1. **Preheat the Oven:**
    - Preheat your oven to 475°F (245°C). If using a pizza stone, place it in the oven to heat up.
2. **Prepare the Natto:**

- Open the natto pack and mix it thoroughly with the soy sauce until creamy. This will enhance its flavor and make it easier to spread over the pizza.
3. **Assemble the Pizza:**
    - Place the pizza crust on a baking sheet or a preheated pizza stone. Spread the tomato sauce evenly over the crust, leaving a small border around the edges.
4. **Add the Toppings:**
    - Sprinkle the sliced onions, bell peppers, mushrooms, and cherry tomatoes over the sauce. Evenly distribute the prepared natto across the pizza.
5. **Top with Cheese:**
    - Generously sprinkle the shredded mozzarella cheese over the vegetables and natto, ensuring even coverage.
6. **Bake the Pizza:**
    - Drizzle olive oil over the top of the pizza and season with salt, pepper, and red pepper flakes if desired. Place in the oven for 12-15 minutes, or until the crust turns golden and the cheese is bubbly with a hint of browning.
7. **Garnish and Serve:**
    - Take the pizza out of the oven and allow it to cool for a few minutes. Top with fresh basil leaves, then cut into slices and serve.

Tips for Preparation:

- **Natto Mixing:** Ensure the natto is well mixed with soy sauce to distribute the flavor evenly across the pizza.
- **Cheese Selection:** For a more robust flavor, try mixing mozzarella with a bit of cheddar or parmesan.
- **Crust Options:** To achieve a crispier crust, bake the dough for a short time before applying the toppings.

Serving Suggestions:

Serve Natto Pizza with a simple green salad or a side of roasted vegetables for a complete meal. Pair it with a light, crisp beer or a chilled white wine to complement the savory flavors. This pizza is perfect for adventurous eaters ready to explore new taste combinations and is sure to be a conversation starter at your next gathering.

Natto & Veggie Wrap

Ingredients:

- 1 pack natto (about 50 grams)
- 4 large whole wheat or spinach tortillas
- 1 tablespoon soy sauce
- 1 tablespoon sesame oil
- 1 cup mixed greens (such as spinach, kale, or arugula)
- 1/2 cucumber, julienned
- 1 carrot, julienned
- 1/4 cup red cabbage, thinly sliced
- 1/4 cup bell pepper, thinly sliced
- 1 avocado, sliced
- 1/4 cup hummus or your favorite spread
- 1 tablespoon sesame seeds

- Salt and pepper to taste
- Fresh cilantro leaves (optional, for garnish)

Instructions:

1. **Prepare the Natto:**
    - Open the natto pack and mix it thoroughly with soy sauce and sesame oil until creamy. This will enhance its flavor and make it easier to spread in the wrap.
2. **Prepare the Vegetables:**
    - Wash and julienne the cucumber and carrot. Thinly slice the red cabbage and bell pepper. Set the vegetables aside.
3. **Assemble the Wrap:**
    - Lay a tortilla flat on a clean surface. Spread a thin layer of hummus across the center, leaving about an inch from the edges.
4. **Add the Fillings:**
    - Arrange a handful of mixed greens over the hummus. Evenly distribute the prepared natto on top, followed by the cucumber, carrot, red cabbage, bell pepper, and avocado slices.
5. **Season and Roll:**
    - Sprinkle sesame seeds, salt, and pepper over the fillings. Roll the tortilla tightly, folding in the sides to secure the fillings.
6. **Slice and Serve:**
    - Cut the wrap in half diagonally for easier handling. Garnish with cilantro leaves if desired.

Tips for Preparation:

- **Natto Mixing:** Ensure the natto is well mixed with soy sauce and sesame oil to spread flavor throughout the wrap.
- **Wrap Handling:** Use fresh, pliable tortillas to prevent tearing. If needed, warm them slightly to make them more flexible.
- **Flavor Boost:** Add a dash of hot sauce or a sprinkle of chili flakes for a spicy kick.

Serving Suggestions:

Serve the Natto & Veggie Wrap with a side of fresh fruit or a light soup for a complete meal. Pair with iced green tea or a refreshing lemonade to complement the flavors. This wrap is ideal for a healthy lunch on-the-go or a light dinner option, ensuring a delightful blend of textures and tastes.

Natto Caesar Salad

Ingredients:

- 1 pack natto (about 50 grams)
- 1 large head of romaine lettuce, chopped
- 1/2 cup croutons
- 1/4 cup grated Parmesan cheese
- 1/4 cup Caesar dressing (store-bought or homemade)
- 1 tablespoon olive oil
- 1 tablespoon lemon juice
- 1 clove garlic, minced
- Salt and pepper to taste

- **Optional:** 1 tablespoon capers, drained
- **Optional:** Anchovy fillets for added flavor

Instructions:

1. **Prepare the Natto:**
   - Open the natto pack and mix it thoroughly with the olive oil and lemon juice to create a creamy consistency. This mixture can be spooned over the salad for a burst of unique flavor.
2. **Prepare the Lettuce:**
   - Wash and dry the romaine lettuce thoroughly. Chop it into bite-sized pieces and place in a large salad bowl.
3. **Mix the Dressing:**
   - If using store-bought Caesar dressing, enhance it by mixing in minced garlic for an extra kick of flavor. If making homemade dressing, combine the dressing ingredients with garlic, salt, and pepper to taste.
4. **Assemble the Salad:**
   - Add the prepared natto mixture to the bowl with lettuce, tossing gently to distribute the natto evenly throughout the salad.
5. **Add Toppings:**
   - Sprinkle croutons and Parmesan cheese over the top. If using, add capers and anchovy fillets for additional depth in flavor.
6. **Dress the Salad:**

- Just before serving, drizzle the Caesar dressing over the salad, tossing until the lettuce is well coated.
7. **Serve:**
   - Transfer the salad to serving plates and garnish with extra Parmesan cheese or a sprinkle of fresh ground pepper for presentation.

Tips for Preparation:

- **Natto Mixing:** Ensure the natto is thoroughly mixed with olive oil and lemon juice for an even, creamy texture that blends well with the salad.
- **Dressing Balance:** Adjust the amount of dressing based on personal preference. Start with a small amount and add more as needed.
- **Crouton Crunch:** For an extra crunch, consider toasting homemade croutons with olive oil and garlic.

Serving Suggestions:

Enjoy this Natto Caesar Salad as a light meal on its own or as a side dish to grilled chicken or fish. Pair it with a crisp white wine or sparkling water with lemon for a refreshing dining experience. Perfect for both adventurous eaters and those new to natto, this salad is sure to become a healthy favorite.

Natto Onigiri

Ingredients:

- 2 cups short-grain sushi rice

- 2 1/2 cups water
- 1 pack natto (about 50 grams)
- 2 tablespoons soy sauce
- 1 tablespoon mirin (optional)
- 1 tablespoon chopped green onions
- Salt to taste
- 2 sheets nori (seaweed), cut into strips
- Sesame seeds for garnish (optional)
- Pickled ginger or pickled plums (umeboshi) for serving (optional)

Instructions:

1. **Cook the Rice:**
   - Rinse the sushi rice under cold water until the water runs clear. Combine the rice and water in a rice cooker or a pot. If using a pot, bring to a boil, then reduce the heat to low, cover, and simmer for about 15 minutes until the water is absorbed and rice is tender. Let it sit covered for an additional 10 minutes to finish steaming.
2. **Prepare the Natto:**
   - Open the natto pack and mix it thoroughly with soy sauce and mirin until creamy. Stir in the chopped green onions. This will create a flavorful filling for the onigiri.
3. **Form the Onigiri:**
   - Wet your hands with water and sprinkle them with a bit of salt to prevent the rice from sticking. Take a handful of rice (about 1/2 cup) and flatten it slightly in your palm.

- Place a spoonful of the natto mixture in the center of the rice. Gently fold the rice around the filling, forming a triangle shape. Press firmly but gently to ensure the rice sticks together and the filling is enclosed.
4. **Wrap with Nori:**
    - Wrap a strip of nori around the bottom of the onigiri, leaving a portion of the rice exposed at the top for easy handling.
5. **Garnish and Serve:**
    - Sprinkle sesame seeds on top of the onigiri for added flavor and texture. Serve with pickled ginger or umeboshi on the side for a traditional touch.

Tips for Preparation:

- **Rice Consistency:** Ensure the rice is sticky enough to hold its shape. If it's too dry, it won't form well; if too wet, it will be mushy.
- **Filling Variations:** Add some chopped shiso leaves or a bit of mustard for a spicy kick to the natto mixture.
- **Shape Options:** Experiment with different shapes, like balls or cylinders, especially if you're making these for kids or bento boxes.

Serving Suggestions:

Enjoy Natto Onigiri as part of a Japanese meal, alongside miso soup and a side of pickled vegetables. They make an excellent portable snack, perfect for picnics or packed lunches. For a refreshing drink pairing, consider green tea to complement the savory flavors.

Natto Stir-fry with Tofu

Ingredients:

- One package of natto (around 50g)
- 200g of firm tofu, pressed and cut into cubes
- 1 tbsp of soy sauce
- 1 tbsp of mirin (optional)
- 2 tbsp of vegetable oil
- 1 clove of garlic, finely minced
- 1-inch piece of ginger, finely minced
- 1 bell pepper, sliced
- 1 cup of broccoli florets
- 1 carrot, cut into julienne strips
- 2 tbsp of chopped spring onions
- 1 tbsp of sesame seeds
- Salt and pepper to your preference
- Cooked rice for serving

Instructions:

1. **Prepare the Tofu:**
   - Press the tofu to remove excess moisture and cut it into cubes. Heat 1 tablespoon of vegetable oil in a non-stick pan over medium heat. Add the tofu cubes, season with salt and pepper, and cook until golden brown on all sides, about 5-7 minutes. Remove and set aside.
2. **Prepare the Natto:**

- In a small bowl, mix the natto with soy sauce and mirin until well combined. This will be added towards the end for a flavor boost.
3. **Stir-fry the Vegetables:**
    - In the same skillet, pour in the leftover tablespoon of oil. Cook the garlic and ginger until they release their aroma. Toss in the bell pepper, broccoli, and carrot, and stir-fry for around 4-5 minutes until the vegetables are just tender yet still crisp.
4. **Combine Ingredients:**
    - Return the tofu to the pan and add the natto mixture. Stir gently to combine everything, allowing the flavors to meld together for another 2 minutes. Adjust seasoning with salt and pepper as needed.
5. **Garnish and Serve:**
    - Sprinkle the stir-fry with sesame seeds and chopped spring onions for added flavor and a touch of color. Serve hot over a bed of steamed rice for a complete meal.

Tips for Preparation:

- **Tofu Texture:** Ensure the tofu is well-pressed to achieve a firmer texture that holds up well in the stir-fry.
- **Natto Flavor:** Mixing natto with soy sauce and mirin can help balance its strong flavor, making it more palatable for those new to natto.

- **Vegetable Variety:** Feel free to add or substitute other vegetables like sugar snap peas or mushrooms to suit your taste preferences.

Serving Suggestions:

This Natto Stir-fry with Tofu pairs well with a side of miso soup or a fresh green salad. For a complete meal, enjoy it with a chilled green tea or a light, fruity white wine. Perfect for a weeknight dinner or a quick lunch, this dish offers a delightful blend of flavors and nutrients, inviting you to enjoy the unique taste of natto in a new and exciting way.

Natto & Egg Breakfast Bowl

Ingredients:

- 1 pack natto (about 50 grams)
- 2 large eggs
- 1 tablespoon soy sauce
- 1/2 teaspoon sesame oil
- 1 cup cooked rice (preferably short grain)
- 1/4 avocado, sliced
- 1 tablespoon chopped green onions
- 1 teaspoon sesame seeds
- Salt and pepper to taste
- **Optional:** chili flakes or hot sauce for a spicy kick

Instructions:

1. **Prepare the Rice:**

- Begin by cooking the rice if it is not already prepared. Use short-grain rice for the best texture. Once cooked, keep it warm.
2. **Cook the Eggs:**
    - Heat a non-stick skillet over medium heat and lightly coat with sesame oil. Crack the eggs into the skillet and cook to your liking, either sunny-side-up or scrambled. Season with salt and pepper. Set aside.
3. **Prepare the Natto:**
    - In a small bowl, mix the natto with soy sauce until well coated. This will enhance the natto's flavor and make it more palatable for those new to it.
4. **Assemble the Bowl:**
    - Place the warm rice in a serving bowl. Arrange the cooked eggs on top, followed by the natto mixture. Add sliced avocado and sprinkle with green onions and sesame seeds for garnish.
5. **Add Final Touches:**
    - For an extra flavor dimension, add a dash of chili flakes or a drizzle of hot sauce if desired. Serve immediately while the ingredients are warm.

Tips for Preparation:

- **Rice Texture:** For a more aromatic flavor, consider using a mix of brown and white rice or adding a dash of rice vinegar to the cooked rice.

- **Egg Options:** Customize the eggs according to your preference—soft-boiled or poached eggs work well with this dish too.
- **Natto Flavor:** If you find natto's flavor strong, try mixing it with a bit of mustard or adding a splash of ponzu sauce for a citrusy boost.

Serving Suggestions:

This Natto & Egg Breakfast Bowl pairs perfectly with a cup of green tea or miso soup for a complete Japanese-inspired breakfast. It's a wholesome way to enjoy the morning, offering a balance of protein and healthy fats to fuel your day. Whether you're a natto novice or an enthusiast, this breakfast bowl delivers a unique and satisfying culinary experience.

Natto Veggie Burger

Ingredients:

- One package of natto (approximately 50g)
- 1 cup of black beans, rinsed and drained
- 1/2 cup of breadcrumbs
- 1/4 cup of onion, finely chopped
- 1/4 cup of carrot, grated
- 1 clove of garlic, minced
- 1 tbsp of soy sauce
- 1 tbsp of olive oil
- 1 tsp of smoked paprika
- 1/2 tsp of cumin
- Salt and pepper, to taste
- 4 whole-grain burger buns

- Lettuce leaves, tomato slices, and avocado for serving
- **Optional:** cheese slices, pickles, or your preferred burger condiments

Instructions:

1. **Prepare the Mixture:**
    - In a large bowl, mash the black beans with a fork or potato masher until mostly smooth, leaving some whole beans for texture. Add the natto, breadcrumbs, onion, carrot, garlic, soy sauce, smoked paprika, cumin, salt, and pepper. Mix until well combined.
2. **Form the Patties:**
    - Divide the mixture into four equal portions and shape each into a patty. Ensure the patties are compact to hold together well while cooking.
3. **Cook the Patties:**
    - Warm olive oil in a non-stick pan over medium heat. Sear the patties for roughly 4-5 minutes per side until they achieve a golden brown color and are thoroughly heated. Carefully flip them to preserve their shape.
4. **Assemble the Burgers:**
    - Toast the burger buns lightly if desired. Place a lettuce leaf on the bottom half of each bun, followed by a natto veggie patty. Top with tomato slices, avocado, and any other desired toppings. Finish with the top half of the bun.

Tips for Preparation:

- **Binding the Mixture:** If the mixture feels too wet, add more breadcrumbs a tablespoon at a time until it holds together well.
- **Flavor Enhancement:** For added flavor, consider incorporating chopped fresh herbs like parsley or cilantro into the patty mixture.
- **Cooking Method:** These patties can also be cooked on a grill pan or baked in the oven at 375°F (190°C) for about 15-20 minutes, flipping halfway through.

Serving Suggestions:

Pair your Natto Veggie Burger with sweet potato fries or a fresh green salad for a balanced meal. A refreshing lemonade or iced tea complements the savory flavors nicely. Whether you're a longtime natto lover or a curious first-timer, this burger offers a deliciously unique taste experience.

Natto Spaghetti

Ingredients:

- 200g of spaghetti
- One pack of natto (approximately 50g)
- 2 tbsp of soy sauce
- 1 tbsp of olive oil
- 1 clove of garlic, minced
- Half an onion, finely diced
- 1/4 cup of Parmesan cheese, grated
- 1 tbsp of butter
- Salt and pepper, to your liking
- 1 tbsp of parsley, chopped, for garnish

- **Optional:** Red pepper flakes

Instructions:

1. **Cook the Spaghetti:**
   - Heat a large pot of salted water until it boils. Add the spaghetti and cook until it reaches an al dente texture, following the package directions. Set aside 1/2 cup of the pasta water, then drain and reserve the pasta.
2. **Prepare the Natto:**
   - In a small bowl, mix the natto with soy sauce until well combined. This mixture will serve as a unique sauce for the pasta.
3. **Sauté the Aromatics:**
   - In a large skillet, heat olive oil over medium heat. Add the garlic and onion, sautéing until the onion becomes translucent and fragrant.
4. **Combine Ingredients:**
   - Add the cooked spaghetti to the skillet, tossing to coat with the garlic and onion mixture. Stir in the natto mixture and butter, adding a splash of reserved pasta water if needed to create a silky sauce. Mix until everything is evenly coated, and the pasta is heated through.
5. **Finish with Cheese:**
   - Sprinkle the grated Parmesan cheese over the pasta, tossing to incorporate. Season with salt, pepper, and red pepper flakes for a spicy kick if desired.
6. **Garnish and Serve:**

- Transfer the natto spaghetti to serving plates and garnish with chopped parsley for a fresh touch.

Tips for Preparation:

- **Pasta Water:** Using reserved pasta water helps the sauce cling better to the spaghetti, enhancing the texture.
- **Flavor Balance:** Adjust the amount of soy sauce and Parmesan to balance the natto's strong flavor to your liking.
- **Additional Toppings:** Consider adding sliced cherry tomatoes or a poached egg on top for extra texture and richness.

Serving Suggestions:

Serve this Natto Spaghetti alongside a crisp green salad or garlic bread for a complete meal. A glass of chilled white wine or a light beer pairs well, complementing the savory notes of the dish. Whether you're a natto enthusiast or trying it for the first time, this recipe offers a delightful and adventurous dining experience.

Conclusion

As you reach the end of this comprehensive guide on natto, it's clear that this traditional Japanese delicacy is more than just an exotic ingredient. Natto embodies a rich cultural heritage, having been a staple in Japanese cuisine for centuries. By delving into its unique preparation and fermentation process, you gain a deeper appreciation for its place in the culinary world. Its distinctive sticky texture, bold aroma, and rich flavor may seem daunting at first, but they hold an allure that many have come to cherish.

Culturally, natto is a symbol of Japanese tradition, especially revered in regions known for its production, like Ibaraki Prefecture. It represents a connection to a time-honored culinary practice, offering you a taste of history with each bite. As you incorporate natto into your meals, you participate in preserving and celebrating this cultural legacy, bringing a piece of Japan's gastronomic identity into your home.

Health-wise, natto is a powerhouse of nutrients, boasting high levels of protein, vitamins, and probiotics. Its cardiovascular benefits, thanks to nattokinase, and its positive impact on bone health due to vitamin K2, make it a worthy addition to your diet. Incorporating natto can enhance your overall wellness, supporting your heart, bones, and digestive system. These benefits, combined with its potential to aid in reducing inflammation and improving gut health, make natto not just a food, but a functional tool in your health regimen.

Culinarily, natto's versatility shines through. Whether you choose to enjoy it traditionally over rice or get creative by incorporating it into salads, omelets, or even smoothies, natto can adapt to various flavors and textures. Its ability to blend into different dishes allows you to experiment and discover new taste experiences, expanding your culinary repertoire. By integrating natto into your meals, you invite a world of new flavors and textures, enhancing your dishes with a unique umami depth and nutritional boost.

As you consider making natto a part of your diet, remember that the journey of incorporating new foods can be gradual and rewarding. Start small, explore combinations with familiar ingredients, and over time, you may find yourself developing a genuine appreciation for its distinct taste and benefits. Embrace the opportunity to widen your culinary horizons and enjoy the health advantages that come with it.

The adventure of discovering natto is as enriching as it is flavorful. Allow yourself to be open to its unique qualities and potential health rewards. Trust your taste buds to guide you on this culinary journey, and don't shy away from experimenting with different recipes and serving styles. By doing so, you'll not only enhance your dietary variety but also gain a deeper understanding and appreciation of this remarkable dish.

So, take this newfound knowledge and confidence, and embark on your own natto exploration. Let it transform from an unfamiliar ingredient into a beloved staple in your kitchen. With each dish, you'll be not just nourishing your body, but also connecting with a rich cultural tradition that spans generations. Embrace natto, and let it become a delicious and healthful part of your culinary story.

FAQs

What is natto and how is it traditionally prepared?

Natto is a traditional Japanese dish made from fermented soybeans. The preparation involves soaking soybeans, cooking them until soft, and then fermenting them with Bacillus subtilis bacteria. Traditionally, the beans were wrapped in rice straw to naturally introduce the bacteria, but modern methods often use a culture starter. The fermentation process lasts 24 to 48 hours, resulting in natto's signature sticky texture and strong aroma.

What are the health benefits of consuming natto?

Natto is packed with health benefits, primarily due to its high levels of protein, probiotics, and vitamin K2. It supports heart health by reducing blood clot formation and lowering blood pressure. The probiotics enhance gut health, while vitamin K2 is essential for bone strength and cardiovascular function. Natto's anti-inflammatory properties and nutrient richness make it a valuable addition to a balanced diet.

How does natto fit into Japanese culture and cuisine?

Natto is deeply rooted in Japanese culture, serving as both a traditional food and a symbol of regional pride, especially in areas like Ibaraki Prefecture. It is commonly enjoyed as a breakfast item over rice and is celebrated for its health benefits and connection to Japanese culinary heritage. Its versatility allows it to be used in various dishes, reflecting the creativity and diversity of Japanese cuisine.

What are some common misconceptions about natto's taste and texture?

Many people find natto's sticky texture and pungent aroma challenging at first. However, these unique characteristics are part of what makes natto distinctive. Its earthy and slightly nutty flavor can become enjoyable over time. Combining natto with familiar foods like rice or using condiments like soy sauce and mustard can help acclimate new eaters to its taste.

How can I incorporate natto into my meals?

Natto can be incorporated into various meals throughout the day. For breakfast, try natto toast or a natto and egg breakfast bowl. At lunch, add it to salads or sushi rolls. For dinner, use natto in stir-fries, pasta dishes, or even as a topping for pizzas. Experimenting with different recipes and familiar ingredients can make natto a regular and enjoyable part of your diet.

Are there any potential disadvantages or side effects of eating natto?

While natto is highly nutritious, it may not appeal to everyone due to its strong flavor and texture. It can also trigger allergies in individuals sensitive to soy. Some commercial varieties have high sodium content, so it's essential to monitor portions. Additionally, natto may be challenging to find in some regions, although online options are increasingly available.

Is making natto at home difficult, and what should I know before trying?

Making natto at home involves a fermenting process that requires time and attention to detail. Key steps include soaking and cooking soybeans, introducing Bacillus subtilis bacteria, and maintaining the right temperature for fermentation. While it can be complex, many people find the effort rewarding. Alternatively, pre-made natto is available in Asian grocery stores, providing a convenient option for those wanting to try it without the hassle of home fermentation.

Resources and Helpful Links

Writer, U. S. (2024, September 4). *What is Natto? The Benefits of Natto and More*. U.S. Soy. https://ussoy.org/what-is-natto-the-benefits-of-natto-and-more/

Rd, A. P. M. (2023, January 11). *Why Natto is super healthy and nutritious*. Healthline. https://www.healthline.com/nutrition/natto

The Ultimate guide to Japanese Natto. (n.d.). https://www.byfood.com/blog/what-is-natto-japanese-fermented-soybeans-p-608

Taste, J. (2024, April 5). *10 unique ways to enjoy natto - easy natto recipes you can make at home*. Japanese Taste. https://int.japanesetaste.com/blogs/japanese-taste-blog/10-unique-ways-to-enjoy-natto-easy-natto-recipes-you-can-make-at-home

Phelps, C. (2024, April 11). *The best Natto recipe*. Pickled Plum. https://pickledplum.com/how-to-eat-natto-natto/

Ellie. (2023, April 28). *Beginner's Guide to Natto*. Ellie Likes Cooking. https://www.cllielikes.cooking/beginners-guide-to-natto/

Taste, J. (2023, January 11). *Everything you need to know about Natto and why you should consume it*. Japanese Taste. https://int.japanesetaste.com/blogs/japanese-taste-blog/everything-you-need-to-know-about-natto-and-why-you-should-con sume-it#:~:text=Natto%20could%20also%20be%20described,slightly%20sweet%2C%20and%20spicy%20flavor.

www.ingramcontent.com/pod-product-compliance
Lightning Source LLC
LaVergne TN
LVHW012036060526
838201LV00061B/4625